Prayers
of
Adoration

EVERYDAY CATHOLIC PRAYERS

Prayer of Adoration to the Holy Spirit

Holy Spirit, Breath of God, I adore You.

Fill me with Your divine presence and guide me in all my ways.

May I be open to Your inspirations and live a life that reflects Your love and truth.

Amen.

Prayer of Adoration to the Creator

Heavenly Father, Creator of all things, I adore You.
Your majesty and power are beyond comprehension.
Help me to see Your hand in all creation and to live
in awe of Your greatness.

Amen.

Prayer of Adoration to the Holy Trinity

O Most Holy Trinity, Father, Son, and Holy Spirit,
I adore You profoundly.
I offer You all the love of my heart and soul.
Grant me the grace to live in Your presence and to
glorify Your holy name in all I do.
Amen.

Prayer of Adoration to the Blessed Sacrament

O Jesus, truly present in the Holy Eucharist,
I adore You with all my heart.
You are the Bread of Life, the Living Bread come
down from heaven.
Nourish my soul with Your divine presence and
make me worthy of Your love.
Amen.

Prayer of Adoration to the Sacred Heart

Sacred Heart of Jesus, burning with love for us,
inflame my heart with the fire of Your divine love.
May I always seek refuge in Your most loving heart
and find peace and consolation in You.

Amen.

Prayer of Adoration to the Holy Cross

O Holy Cross, on which the Savior of the world was
crucified, I adore You.

Through Your sacrifice, You brought salvation to all.

Help me to embrace my own crosses with faith and
to follow Jesus in His suffering.

Amen.

Prayers
of
Thanksgiving

EVERYDAY CATHOLIC PRAYERS

Thanksgiving for Daily Blessings

Heavenly Father, I thank You for all the blessings of
this day.
Thank You for the gift of life, for my family and
friends, for the food I eat and the air I breathe.
May I never take Your gifts for granted.
Amen.

Thanksgiving for the Sacraments

O Lord, I thank You for the grace of the sacraments.
Thank You for the gift of Baptism, which made me
Your child, for Confirmation, which strengthened
me with Your Spirit, and for the Holy Eucharist,
where I receive Your Body and Blood.
Amen.

Thanksgiving for Healing

Lord Jesus, I thank You for the healing You have
brought into my life.
Whether physical, emotional, or spiritual, Your
touch has restored me.
Help me to always trust in Your healing power and
to be grateful for Your mercy.
Amen.

Thanksgiving for Forgiveness

Merciful Father, I thank You for the forgiveness of
my sins.

Your mercy is boundless and Your love is
everlasting.

Help me to live in the freedom of Your grace and to
forgive others as You have forgiven me.

Amen.

Thanksgiving for Family

Heavenly Father, I thank You for the gift of my
family.
For their love, support, and presence in my life, I am
deeply grateful.
Bless each member of my family and keep us united
in Your love.
Amen.

Thanksgiving for God's Guidance

Lord, I thank You for guiding me through the
challenges and decisions of life.
Your wisdom has led me on the right path.
Help me to always seek Your guidance and to trust
in Your divine plan.
Amen.

Prayers
of
Petition

EVERYDAY CATHOLIC PRAYERS

Prayer for Guidance

Holy Spirit, guide me in all my decisions.
Illuminate my mind and fill my heart with wisdom.
Help me to discern Your will in every situation and
to follow the path that leads to You.

Amen.

Prayer for
Strength

Lord Jesus, grant me the strength to face the
challenges of this day.
Help me to carry my cross with patience and to find
comfort in Your love.
May Your strength sustain me in moments of
weakness.
Amen.

Prayer for Forgiveness

Merciful Father, I come before You with a contrite
heart.
Forgive me for my sins and help me to forgive those
who have hurt me.
Cleanse me with Your grace and lead me to the path
of righteousness.
Amen.

Prayer for
Protection

Guardian Angel, watch over me and protect me
from all harm.
Keep me safe from danger and lead me on the path
of righteousness.
May I always feel your comforting presence by my
side.
Amen.

Prayer for Peace

Lord Jesus, Prince of Peace, grant us peace in our hearts, in our homes, and in our world.
Help us to be peacemakers and to work towards reconciliation and justice.
Amen.

Prayer for Wisdom

Heavenly Father, grant me the wisdom to make the right choices in life.

Help me to seek Your will in all I do and to follow the path that leads to eternal life.

Amen.

Prayers
of
Intercession

EVERYDAY CATHOLIC PRAYERS

Intercession for Families

Holy Family of Nazareth, bless and protect all families.

Grant us unity, peace, and love.

Help us to follow your example of faithfulness and devotion.

May our homes be places of prayer and mutual support.

Amen.

Intercession for the Sick

O Lord, we pray for those who are sick and
suffering.
Grant them healing and relief from their pain.
Comfort them with Your presence and give strength
to those who care for them.
Amen.

Intercession for the Departed

Eternal Father, we pray for the souls of our departed
loved ones.

Grant them eternal rest and let perpetual light shine
upon them.

May they find peace in Your loving embrace.

Amen.

Intercession for the Church

Lord Jesus, we pray for Your Church.
Bless and guide our Pope, bishops, priests, and all
who serve in Your name.
Grant them the strength and wisdom to lead us in
faith and holiness.
Amen.

Intercession for Our Nation

Heavenly Father, we pray for our nation and its leaders.

Grant them wisdom and courage to make just and compassionate decisions.

Help us to work together for the common good and to promote peace and justice.

Amen.

Intercession for Vocations

Heavenly Father, call forth from our community
faithful and dedicated servants to Your Church.
Grant us priests, deacons, and religious who will lead
us in holiness and guide us to Your kingdom.
Amen.

Prayers
for
Daily Life

EVERYDAY CATHOLIC PRAYERS

Prayer of the Morning

Lord, as I begin this day, I offer You all my thoughts, words, and actions.

Guide me and give me the strength to do Your will.

May this day be filled with Your grace and blessings.

Amen

Prayer of the

Evening

Heavenly Father, as the day comes to an end, I thank
You for Your many blessings.

Forgive me for any wrongs I have done and grant
me a restful night.

May I awaken refreshed and ready to serve You.

Amen.

Prayer before Meals

Bless us, O Lord, and these Thy gifts which we are about to receive from Thy bounty.

Through Christ our Lord.

Amen.

Prayer after Meals

We give You thanks, Almighty God, for all Your benefits, who lives and reigns, world without end. Amen.

Prayer for Work

Lord, bless the work of my hands today.
Help me to do my tasks with diligence and integrity.
May my work be a reflection of Your love and bring glory to Your name.
Amen.

Prayer for Travel

O God, protect me as I travel today.

Keep me safe from harm and bring me to my
destination in peace.

May Your angels watch over me and guide my way.

Amen.

Made in the USA
Las Vegas, NV
28 November 2024

12841944R00023